Maths at Work

Maths at the Shops

Tracey Steffora

Raintree

Raintree is an imprint of Capstone Global Library Limited, a company incorporated in England and Wales having its registered office at 7 Pilgrim Street, London, EC4V 6LB – Registered company number: 6695582

To contact Raintree please phone 0845 6044371, fax + 44 (0) 1865 312263, or email myorders@ raintreepublishers.co.uk. Customers from outside the UK please telephone +44 1865 312262.

Edited by Dan Nunn and Abby Colich
Designed by Victoria Allen
Picture research by Tracy Cummins
Production control by Victoria Fitzgerald
Printed and bound in China by Leo Paper Products Ltd

ISBN 978 1 406 25073 2
16 15 14 13 12
10 9 8 7 6 5 4 3 2 1

British Library Cataloguing in Publication Data
Steffora, Tracey.
Maths at the shops. – (Maths at work)
510-dc23
A full catalogue record for this book is available from the British Library.

Acknowledgements
We would like to thank the following for permission to reproduce photographs: Corbis: pp. 6 (© Glowimages), 7 (© Lew Robertson), 10 (© Hola Images), 11 (© Rob Melnychu), 14 (© Lucas Tange/cultura), 17 (© Marc Leon/ cultura), 20 (© Helen King), 22 (© Lew Robertson); Getty Images: pp. 8 (Ariel Skelley), 12 (gerenme), 21 (Purestock); iStockphoto: pp. 15 (© Leontura), 16 (© Catherine Yeulet), 18 (© Linda Steward); Shutterstock: pp. 4 (Kenneth Sponsler), 5 (Tyler Olson), 9 (Kzenon), 13 (Wutthichai), 19 (Robert Kneschke).

Front cover photograph of a shop worker in a supermarket reproduced with permission from Getty Images (Fuse).

Back cover photograph of a tailor in a shop measuring the length of a man's arm reproduced with permission from iStockphoto (© Leontura).

Every effort has been made to contact copyright holders of any material reproduced in this book. Any omissions will be rectified in subsequent printings if notice is given to the publisher.

Contents

Maths at the shops

There are many types of shops.

People buy things in shops.

People use maths in shops.

Counting

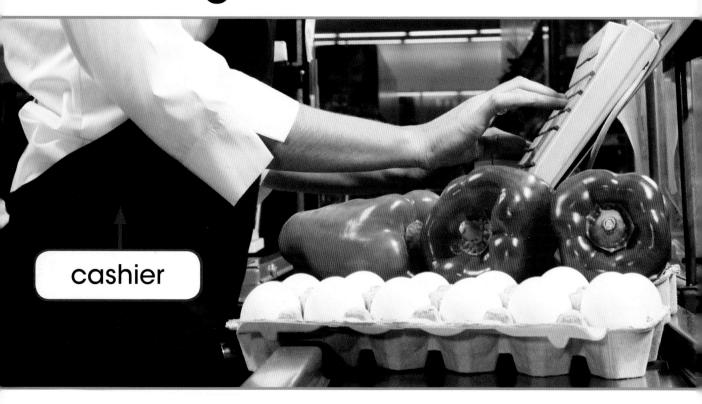

cashier

The cashier counts items.

The cashier counts money.

baker

The baker counts cakes
and biscuits.

How many loaves of bread can you count? (answer on page 22)

Sorting

This man sorts by size.

This man sorts by colour.

This woman sorts by shape.

How would you sort these watches?

(answer on page 22)

Measuring

scales

This man measures how heavy things are.

This man measures how tall
people are.

This woman measures how much coffee to put in the cups.

Are these people measuring
how long or how heavy?

(answer on page 22)

17

Shapes

triangle

There are many shapes in shops.

This woman is holding a square box.

circle

This bicycle wheel is a circle.

What shape is the bag?

(answer on page 22)

JN/22596

Answers

page 9: There are two loaves of bread.

page 13: You would sort them by colour.

page 17: They are measuring how long.

page 21: The shape is a rectangle.

Picture glossary

cashier person who takes money when you pay for something. Many cashiers work in shops.

Index

Notes for parents and teachers

Maths is a way that we make sense of the world around us. For the young child, this includes recognizing similarities and differences, classifying objects, recognizing shapes and patterns, developing number sense, and using simple measurement skills.

Before reading

Connect with what children know

Ask children to name different types of shops, and make a list (supermarket, bakery, clothes shop, etc.). Ask them to think of things that need to be counted when shopping in a shop or market (fruit, vegetables, tins, money, etc.).

After reading

Build upon children's curiosity and desire to explore

• For parents, involve children in counting, measuring, or sorting items while on shopping trips. Giving them real world experience with maths in their environment will help lay the groundwork for further mathematical growth and development.

• In the classroom, provide experiences for children to sort and classify items, such as types of fruit, vegetables, buttons, or coins.